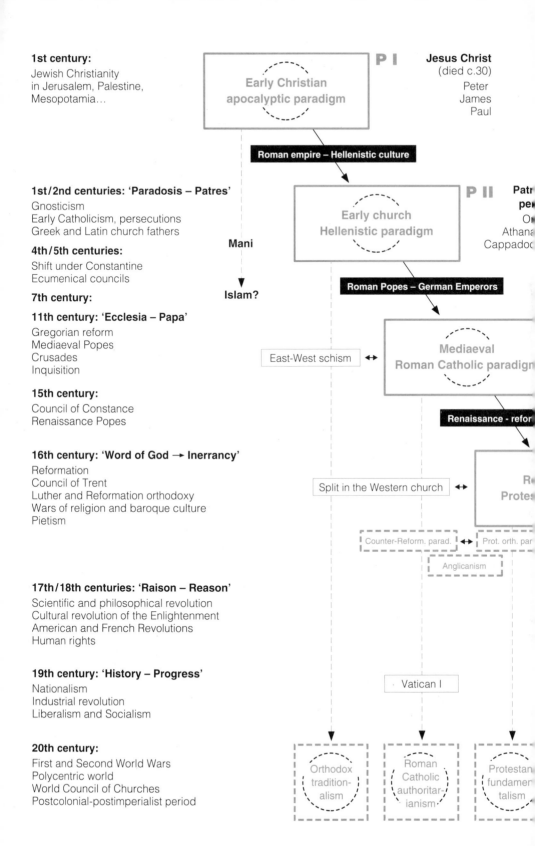

1st century:
Jewish Christianity
in Jerusalem, Palestine,
Mesopotamia...

1st/2nd centuries: 'Paradosis – Patres'
Gnosticism
Early Catholicism, persecutions
Greek and Latin church fathers

4th/5th centuries:
Shift under Constantine
Ecumenical councils

7th century:

11th century: 'Ecclesia – Papa'
Gregorian reform
Mediaeval Popes
Crusades
Inquisition

15th century:
Council of Constance
Renaissance Popes

16th century: 'Word of God → Inerrancy'
Reformation
Council of Trent
Luther and Reformation orthodoxy
Wars of religion and baroque culture
Pietism

17th/18th centuries: 'Raison – Reason'
Scientific and philosophical revolution
Cultural revolution of the Enlightenment
American and French Revolutions
Human rights

19th century: 'History – Progress'
Nationalism
Industrial revolution
Liberalism and Socialism

20th century:
First and Second World Wars
Polycentric world
World Council of Churches
Postcolonial-postimperialist period

P I

Jesus Christ
(died c.30)
Peter
James
Paul

Early Christian
apocalyptic paradigm

Roman empire – Hellenistic culture

P II   Patr
pe
O
Athana
Cappado

Early church
Hellenistic paradigm

Mani

Islam?

Roman Popes – German Emperors

East-West schism ↔

Mediaeval
Roman Catholic paradigm

Renaissance - refor

Split in the Western church ↔

R
Prote

Counter-Reform. parad. ↔ Prot. orth. par

Anglicanism

Vatican I

Orthodox
tradition-
alism

Roman
Catholic
authoritar-
ianism

Protestan
fundamen
talism

Paradigm Shifts in Christianity

The abiding substance of faith:

The message: 'Jesus the Christ'.
The decisive event of revelation, the turning point in the history
of Israel as a result of the coming of Jesus of Nazareth.
The distinctive Christian element: **Jesus** as God's **Messiah** and **Son.**

The shifting paradigm (=P)
(macromodel of society, religion, theology):

Augustine
Leo I
Gregory I

'An entire constellation of beliefs, values, techniques which are shared by
the members of a particular community' (Thomas S. Kuhn).

P III   Scholasticism:
Thomas
Bonaventure

ncils

P IV   Reformation:
Luther / Erasmus
Zwingli-Calvin
Cranmer

nation
paradigm

**Modern philosophy,
natural sciences, theory of the state**

**P V   Enlightenment
and Idealism:**
Schleiermacher
liberal theology
Harnack

Enlightenment
modern paradigm

**Industrialization
democratization**

Vatican II

Liberal
modernism

Contemporary
ecumenical paradigm
(postmodern) ?

P VI

Christianity

THE RELIGIOUS SITUATION OF OUR TIME

Christianity

No peace among the nations
without peace among the religions.

No peace among the religions
without dialogue between the religions.

No dialogue between the religions
without investigation of the foundation of the religions.